Unleashing the Inner Fire: The Ancient Art of

Tummo Breathwork for Radical Transformation

Emily K Patel

Forbidden Mantra Press

Table of Contents: Tummo - The Inner Fire

Breathing Technique

1. Introduction to Tummo

1.1 Origins and Background

Tummo has its roots in the ancient traditions of Tibetan Buddhism. The practice is deeply intertwined with the spiritual and philosophical teachings of this tradition. The term "Tummo" itself translates to "inner fire" in Tibetan, and it refers to the generation and harnessing of an internal heat that can be experienced through specific breathing techniques, visualization, and meditation.

The origins of Tummo can be traced back to the teachings of the ancient Indian yogic practices, particularly the practices of pranayama (breath control) and Kundalini Yoga. These practices were introduced to Tibet through the influence of great Indian yogis and masters, such as Padmasambhava and Naropa, during the eighth and eleventh centuries.

In Tibetan Buddhism, Tummo is considered a profound and advanced practice that is typically taught within the context of specific spiritual lineages, such as the Mahamudra and Dzogchen traditions. It is often associated with the Vajrayana or Tantric path, which emphasizes the transformation of ordinary experiences into spiritual realization.

The practice of Tummo is believed to have been transmitted from master to disciple in an unbroken lineage for centuries. The techniques and teachings were carefully guarded and passed down orally to ensure their purity and integrity.

Traditionally, Tummo was practiced by yogis and monks living in the remote regions of the Himalayas, who dedicated their lives to intensive meditation and spiritual pursuits. These practitioners would engage in extended periods of solitary retreats, during which they would delve deep into the practices of Tummo to unlock the potential for spiritual awakening and enlightenment.

In recent years, the practice of Tummo has gained wider recognition and interest beyond the confines of the Tibetan Buddhist monastic community. It has piqued the curiosity of researchers and scientists who have conducted studies to explore its physiological and psychological effects. Additionally, Tummo has attracted the attention of individuals seeking personal growth, well-being, and spiritual development in various parts of the world.

Today, Tummo is often taught by qualified teachers and practitioners outside of the traditional monastic setting. Workshops, retreats, and training programs are offered to those who wish to learn and explore the profound transformative potential of this ancient breathing technique. However, it is important to approach Tummo practice with respect, guidance, and a deep understanding of its spiritual and cultural context.

1.2 Significance in Tibetan Buddhist Practices

Tummo holds significant importance within the framework of Tibetan Buddhist practices. It is considered a profound and advanced technique that is believed to facilitate spiritual transformation and realization. Here are some key aspects highlighting the significance of Tummo in Tibetan Buddhist traditions:

1. Awakening Inner Wisdom and Enlightenment: Tummo practice is seen as a powerful method for awakening the dormant spiritual potential within an individual. By generating the inner fire and harnessing it through breath control, visualization, and meditation, practitioners aim to purify their body and mind, dissolve mental obscurations, and awaken their innate wisdom and enlightened nature.

2. Purification and Balancing of Energies:

    Tummo is viewed as a transformative process that purifies and balances the subtle energy channels and centers within the body, known as "nadis" and "chakras" respectively. By working with the breath and visualization techniques, practitioners aim to remove blockages, dissolve negative patterns, and harmonize the flow of energy, leading to greater vitality, health, and spiritual well-being.

3. Subtle Body and Inner Heat: Within the framework of Tibetan Buddhist teachings, Tummo is closely associated with the subtle body, which consists of various energy channels, winds, and drops. The generation of inner heat through Tummo practice is believed to awaken and stimulate the subtle energy systems, allowing practitioners to gain

direct experiences of the body-mind connection and transcend ordinary perceptions of reality.

4. Enhancing Meditation and Mindfulness: Tummo serves as a complementary practice to meditation and mindfulness techniques in Tibetan Buddhism. The generation of inner heat can support practitioners in stabilizing their attention, developing mental clarity, and cultivating deep states of concentration. The

heightened bodily awareness and the internal heat generated through Tummo practice can serve as valuable anchors for meditative absorption and insight.

5. Transformation of Emotions and Subtle Forces: Tummo practice is also regarded as a means to transform and harness the powerful energies of emotions, desires, and subtle forces. By engaging with the inner fire, practitioners aim to transmute and redirect

these forces toward spiritual growth, compassion, and altruistic actions. Tummo can be seen as a path to harnessing and integrating the energies of passion, desire, and attachment for spiritual awakening and the benefit of all beings.

6. Lineage Transmission and Guru-Student Relationship: Tummo practice is traditionally transmitted within the context of a lineage, with teachings passed down from qualified

masters to their dedicated disciples. The relationship between the teacher (guru) and the student is highly regarded, and the transmission of Tummo often involves not only the teachings but also the blessings, guidance, and personal connection between the teacher and student.

Overall, Tummo holds a deep significance in Tibetan Buddhist practices as a transformative and awakening technique. It encompasses the cultivation of inner heat, purification of energies, enhancement of meditation, and the integration of emotions and subtle forces. The practice of Tummo is deeply interwoven with the broader spiritual path of Tibetan Buddhism, offering practitioners a means to awaken their true nature and attain spiritual liberation.

Chapter 2: Understanding the Inner Fire

2.1 Concept of Inner Fire in Tibetan Buddhism

In Tibetan Buddhism, the concept of inner fire, referred to as "Tummo," holds profound significance. It is considered a metaphorical and experiential representation of the subtle energy and transformative potential within the practitioner. Understanding the concept of inner fire is essential to grasp the depth and purpose of Tummo practice. Here's an exploration of the concept:

The Subtle Energy System: Tibetan Buddhist teachings describe a subtle energy system within the human body. It consists of channels (nadis), winds (prana or lung), and energy centers (chakras). These channels and winds are responsible for the flow of energy throughout the body, while the energy centers act as focal points for specific qualities and states of consciousness.

Awakening the Inner Fire: Within this subtle energy system, the inner fire represents a dormant potential. It is likened to a hidden flame waiting to be kindled. Through the practice of Tummo, practitioners aim to awaken and cultivate this inner fire, allowing it to blaze brightly, illuminating their spiritual path.

The Transformation of Winds: The winds (prana or lung) are considered the carriers of energy within the body. They are responsible for various physiological and psychological functions. In Tummo practice, specific breath control techniques are employed to regulate and redirect the flow of winds. By harnessing and channeling the winds, practitioners aim to awaken and intensify the inner fire.

The Central Channel and Kundalini Energy:

Tibetan Buddhist teachings also emphasize the central channel, known as "sushumna," which runs along the spine. It is believed to be the main conduit for the movement of energy and the primary seat of the inner fire. In Tummo practice, the awakening of the inner fire is associated with the activation of the central channel and the ascent of the Kundalini energy, which represents the latent spiritual potential residing at the base of the spine.

Transmutation of Dualistic Perception: The concept of inner fire in Tibetan Buddhism goes beyond its physiological and energetic aspects. It also holds significance in terms of transforming one's perception of reality. It is believed that through the practice of Tummo and the awakening of the inner fire, practitioners can dissolve dualistic perceptions and experience the interconnectedness and non-dual nature of existence.

Symbolism of Transformation and Purification: The inner fire is often depicted symbolically as a flaming triangular shape, representing transformation and purification. It symbolizes the burning away of negative emotions, obscurations, and habitual patterns that hinder spiritual progress. The heat generated through Tummo practice is seen as a purifying force that facilitates the purification and transformation of body, mind, and consciousness.

Integration of Inner Fire with Wisdom: In Tibetan Buddhism, the inner fire is considered inseparable from wisdom. It is believed that as the inner fire blazes brighter, it illuminates the practitioner's understanding, insight, and realization. The integration of the inner fire with wisdom leads to the direct experience of the true nature of reality and the awakening of enlightened qualities.

By understanding the concept of inner fire in Tibetan Buddhism, practitioners of Tummo gain insight into the profound symbolism and transformative potential of this practice. It signifies the awakening and cultivation of the dormant spiritual energy within, leading to purification, transformation, and the realization of one's true nature.

Chapter 2: Understanding Inner Fire

2.2 Inner Heat and Its Benefits

Within the practice of Tummo in Tibetan Buddhism, the cultivation of inner heat holds significant benefits for practitioners. This inner heat, also known as "Tummo" or "candali," is generated through specific breathing techniques, visualization, and meditation. Understanding the concept of inner heat and its associated benefits is essential to comprehending the transformative potential of Tummo practice. This chapter explores the advantages and effects of cultivating inner heat.

1. Physical Benefits:

1.1 Enhanced Circulation and Vitality: Tummo practice involves the activation and stimulation of the body's subtle energy channels, resulting in improved blood circulation. Increased circulation supports the efficient delivery of oxygen, nutrients, and vital energy to the body's cells, enhancing overall physical health and vitality.

1.2 Regulation of Body Temperature: Through Tummo practice, practitioners develop the ability to generate and regulate their body temperature. This skill becomes particularly valuable in extreme environmental conditions, such as cold climates. By harnessing the inner heat, practitioners can maintain a comfortable body temperature, potentially reducing the risks of hypothermia or heat-related conditions.

1.3 Strengthened Immune System: The cultivation of inner heat is believed to have a positive impact on the immune system. Increased heat and energy generated through Tummo practice can contribute to a strengthened immune response, potentially supporting the body's ability to fight off infections and diseases.

1.4 Improved Energy and Vitality: The generation of inner heat helps to revitalize the body's energy reserves. Practitioners often report experiencing increased levels of energy, endurance, and vitality as a result of regular Tummo practice. This enhanced energy can translate into improved physical performance and overall well-being.

2. Mental and Emotional Benefits:

2.1 Enhanced Mental Clarity and Focus: The practice of Tummo and the cultivation of inner heat are closely linked to mental clarity and focus. As the inner heat intensifies, practitioners often experience heightened levels of concentration and mindfulness. This enhanced mental state can lead to improved cognitive function, increased mental clarity, and sharper focus.

2.2 Emotional Balance and Stability: Tummo practice can have a profound impact on emotional well-being. By working with the inner heat and the

subtle energy system, practitioners often report a

greater sense of emotional balance, stability, and

resilience. The cultivation of inner heat can help to

dissolve emotional blockages, alleviate stress, and

foster a more equanimous and compassionate

approach to life's challenges.

3. Spiritual Benefits:

3.1 Awakening Wisdom and Insight

The cultivation of inner heat within the framework of Tummo practice is deeply intertwined with the awakening of wisdom and insight. As practitioners engage with the inner fire, they may experience profound moments of clarity and direct realization of the nature of reality. This deepening of wisdom and insight paves the way for spiritual growth and the realization of one's true nature.

3.2 Transformation and Spiritual Awakening:

Tummo practice is regarded as a powerful tool for transformation and spiritual awakening. The generation of inner heat can facilitate the purification of negative patterns, obscurations, and habitual tendencies that hinder spiritual progress. Through the integration of the inner fire with wisdom, practitioners can experience profound shifts in consciousness, leading to spiritual growth, liberation, and the embodiment of awakened qualities.

By understanding the benefits associated with the cultivation of inner heat, practitioners of Tummo gain insight into the transformative power of this practice. The physical benefits encompass improved circulation, body temperature regulation, enhanced vitality, and a strengthened immune system. The mental and emotional benefits include increased mental clarity, focus, emotional balance, and stability. The spiritual benefits encompass the awakening of wisdom, insight, transformation, and spiritual awakening. These benefits collectively contribute to the holistic well-being and spiritual development of the practitioner.

Chapter 3: Techniques and Practices

Chapter 3: Techniques and Practices

3.1 Breath Control Methods

Within the practice of Tummo in Tibetan Buddhism, breath control plays a vital role in cultivating inner heat and harnessing the transformative potential of the inner fire. This chapter explores various breath control methods used in Tummo practice, with a focus on deep belly breathing.

3.1.1 Deep Belly Breathing

Deep belly breathing, also known as diaphragmatic breathing or abdominal breathing, is a foundational breath control technique employed in Tummo practice. It involves consciously directing the breath into the lower abdomen, engaging the diaphragm and expanding the belly with each inhalation. Here is an exploration of the practice and its benefits:

1. Technique:

    - Find a comfortable seated position, with an upright posture and relaxed shoulders.

    - Place your hands on your abdomen, just below the navel, to feel the movement of the belly.

- Take a slow and deep inhalation through the nose, allowing the breath to fill the lower abdomen. Feel the expansion of the belly as the diaphragm descends.

- Exhale slowly through the nose, allowing the belly to naturally contract as the diaphragm rises.

- Repeat this deep belly breathing pattern, maintaining a slow and rhythmic pace.

2. Benefits:

- Deepens the Breath: Deep belly breathing allows for a fuller and more expansive breath, engaging the diaphragm and utilizing the full capacity of the lungs. This promotes increased oxygen intake and optimal oxygenation of the body's cells, enhancing overall vitality and well-being.

- Calms the Nervous System: Deep belly breathing activates the parasympathetic nervous system, often referred to as the "rest and digest" response. This induces a relaxation response, reducing stress, anxiety, and the activation of the sympathetic nervous system ("fight or flight" response).

- Enhances Mind-Body Connection: By consciously directing the breath into the lower abdomen, deep belly breathing cultivates a heightened awareness of the body's sensations and the intimate connection between the breath and the physical body. This deepened mind-body connection can support a deeper meditation practice and facilitate the integration of Tummo techniques.

- Facilitates Energy Flow: Deep belly breathing helps to regulate and balance the flow of subtle energy (prana or lung) within the body. By engaging the diaphragm and expanding the belly, the breath assists in clearing blockages and promoting the smooth movement of energy through the energy channels (nadis).

- Supports Inner Heat Generation: Deep belly breathing is an essential component in generating the inner heat required for Tummo practice. By focusing the breath in the lower abdomen and engaging the diaphragm, practitioners create the necessary conditions for harnessing and intensifying the inner fire.

☐ Cultivates Mindfulness and Presence: Deep belly breathing serves as an anchor for cultivating mindfulness and present-moment awareness. By directing attention to the sensations of the breath and the movement of the abdomen, practitioners develop a deeper sense of presence and concentration, enhancing their overall meditative experience.

Deep belly breathing is a foundational breath control technique in Tummo practice. Its benefits encompass deepening the breath, calming the nervous system, enhancing the mind-body connection, facilitating energy flow, supporting inner heat generation, and cultivating mindfulness and presence. Practitioners can incorporate this technique into their Tummo practice to lay a solid foundation for further exploration and transformation.

Chapter 3: Techniques and Practices

In the practice of Tummo, various techniques and practices are employed to cultivate and harness the inner fire. This chapter explores some of the key techniques and practices utilized in Tummo practice, providing insights into their application and benefits.

3.1 Breath Control Methods

Breath control methods play a crucial role in Tummo practice, as they regulate the flow of energy and facilitate the generation of inner heat. Here are some commonly used breath control techniques:

3.1.1 Deep Belly Breathing: Deep belly breathing, also known as diaphragmatic breathing or abdominal breathing, involves directing the breath into the lower abdomen, expanding the belly with each inhalation. This technique allows for a fuller breath, enhances oxygenation, calms the nervous system, and supports the generation of inner heat.

3.1.2 Alternate Nostril Breathing: Alternate nostril breathing is a technique that involves alternating the breath between the left and right nostrils. By regulating the flow of breath through the nadis (subtle energy channels), this practice balances the energy within the body, harmonizes the left and right hemispheres of the brain, and cultivates a sense of inner equilibrium.

3.1.3 Kapalabhati Pranayama: Kapalabhati, or "skull shining breath," is a forceful and rapid exhalation followed by a passive inhalation. This technique helps to cleanse the respiratory system, invigorate the body, and generate inner heat. It also enhances mental clarity and energizes the mind.

3.2 Visualization Techniques

Visualization techniques are used in Tummo practice to enhance the activation and direction of energy within the body. Here are two common visualization techniques:

3.2.1 Inner Fire Visualization: In this technique, practitioners visualize a radiant flame or intense heat residing at the area below the navel, known as the "lower energy center." They imagine this inner fire growing brighter and expanding, gradually filling the entire body with warmth and light. This visualization aids in the awakening and intensification of the inner fire.

3.2.2 Channel Visualization: This technique involves visualizing the subtle energy channels (nadis) within the body. Practitioners imagine these channels as clear and unobstructed pathways through which the energy can freely flow. By visualizing the smooth movement of energy through the channels, practitioners support the circulation and balance of energy throughout the body.

3.3 Meditation and Mindfulness

Meditation and mindfulness are integral aspects of Tummo practice. By cultivating focused attention and present-moment awareness, practitioners deepen their connection with the inner fire and the transformative potential it holds. Here are some meditation and mindfulness practices utilized in Tummo:

3.3.1 Concentration Meditation: Concentration meditation involves focusing the mind on a single object, such as the breath, a visual image, or a mantra. By developing sustained concentration, practitioners refine their ability to direct and control their attention, leading to increased stability of mind and deepening of the Tummo practice.

3.3.2 Body Scan Meditation: Body scan meditation involves systematically bringing mindful attention to different parts of the body. Practitioners observe sensations, tensions, and energy flow within each body part, fostering a deeper embodiment and awareness of the inner fire as it moves through the body.

3.3.3 Mindful Movement: Mindful movement practices, such as yoga or qigong, can be integrated into Tummo practice. By engaging in slow, deliberate movements with awareness, practitioners cultivate a deeper connection between the body, breath, and inner fire. This enhances the integration of Tummo techniques and promotes a sense of fluidity and harmony.

By incorporating these techniques and practices into their Tummo practice, practitioners can deepen their understanding of the inner fire, refine their ability to generate and control inner heat, and experience the transformative power of Tummo on physical, mental, and spiritual levels.

Chapter 4: Generating Inner Heat

In the practice of Tummo, the generation of inner heat, also known as the inner fire, is a fundamental objective. This chapter explores the techniques and methods employed to cultivate and intensify the inner heat, allowing practitioners to tap into its transformative power.

4.1 Purification Practices

Before embarking on the generation of inner heat, it is often recommended to engage in purification practices. These practices aim to cleanse the body, energy channels, and mind, creating optimal conditions for the cultivation of inner heat. Some common purification practices include:

4.1.1 Physical Purification: This involves adopting a clean and healthy lifestyle, maintaining proper hygiene, and engaging in practices such as fasting, detoxification, and dietary adjustments. Physical purification helps to remove toxins from the body and establish a balanced and receptive vessel for the inner fire.

4.1.2 Mental Purification: Mental purification practices involve mindfulness, meditation, and contemplation to cleanse the mind of negative thoughts, emotions, and mental patterns. By cultivating a calm and clear mind, practitioners create a conducive inner environment for the generation and control of inner heat.

4.1.3 Energy Channel Purification

Energy channel purification techniques, such as pranayama (breath control) and subtle energy practices, aim to clear blockages and balance the flow of energy within the body. This ensures the smooth movement of energy through the channels, facilitating the circulation and intensification of inner heat.

4.2 Visualization and Conscious Intention

Visualization techniques are crucial in generating and directing the inner heat. By combining the power of imagination with conscious intention, practitioners can amplify the intensity and focus of the inner fire. Here are some visualization practices used to generate inner heat:

4.2.1 Inner Fire Visualization: As mentioned earlier, the visualization of an inner fire residing in the lower energy center is a key technique. Practitioners visualize the flame growing brighter and expanding, filling the entire body with radiant heat. The conscious intention to awaken and intensify the inner fire enhances the effectiveness of this visualization.

4.2.2 Channel Visualization: Visualizing the energy channels as clear and unobstructed pathways allows the inner heat to flow freely throughout the body. Practitioners imagine the inner fire moving along the channels, dissolving any blockages or impurities it encounters. This visualization supports the smooth circulation and intensification of the inner heat.

4.3 Breath Control Techniques

Breath control techniques are central to generating inner heat in Tummo practice. By manipulating the breath, practitioners can influence the flow of energy and intensify the inner fire. Here are some breath control techniques used for generating inner heat:

4.3.1 Forceful Exhalation: This technique involves forcefully exhaling through the nose, contracting the abdominal muscles to expel the breath. The rapid exhalation stimulates the energy flow and generates heat within the body. It is often combined with visualization and conscious intention to enhance its effectiveness.

4.3.2 Vase Breath: Vase breath, also known as "Ujjayi" or "Victorious breath," involves a slight contraction of the glottis during both inhalation and exhalation, creating a subtle sound in the throat. This breath control technique builds heat and energy within the body, supporting the generation of inner heat.

4.4 Meditation and Focus

Meditation and focused attention play a vital role in generating and sustaining the inner heat. By training the mind to remain focused on the inner fire, practitioners cultivate the ability to increase its intensity and prolong its presence. Here are some meditation practices used in Tummo:

4.4.1 Inner Fire Meditation: Inner fire meditation involves directing one's attention inward, towards the inner fire. Practitioners cultivate a deep focus and concentration on the sensations, heat, and energy associated with the inner fire. This sustained focus allows for the intensification and expansion of the inner heat.

4.4.2 Single-Pointed Concentration: This meditation practice involves focusing the mind on a single point, such as a visual image, a mantra, or the breath. By training the mind to remain concentrated and undistracted, practitioners develop the ability to channel their energy and focus into generating and sustaining the inner heat.

By incorporating these techniques and practices into their Tummo practice, practitioners can gradually generate and amplify the inner heat, experiencing its transformative effects on the body, mind, and spiritual development. It is important to approach these practices with guidance from qualified teachers and with respect for individual abilities and limitations.

Chapter 5: Physical and Mental Transformation

In the practice of Tummo, the cultivation of the inner fire leads to profound physical and mental transformation. This chapter explores the transformative effects that arise as a result of working with the inner heat.

5.1 Physical Transformation

The generation and intensification of the inner heat in Tummo practice have significant physical impacts on the practitioner's body. Here are some key aspects of physical transformation that can occur:

5.1.1 Increased Body Heat: As the inner fire is cultivated and intensified, practitioners may experience a notable increase in body heat. This heightened heat can permeate the entire body, creating a sensation of warmth and radiance. It can support various physiological processes, enhance metabolism, and promote overall vitality.

5.1.2 Improved Energy Circulation: The inner fire generated through Tummo practice helps to clear energy blockages and balance the flow of subtle energy (prana or lung) within the body. This balanced energy circulation optimizes the functioning of the body's systems, promotes healing, and enhances overall well-being.

5.1.3 Enhanced Immune System: The cultivation of inner heat can have positive effects on the immune system. The increased body heat and improved energy circulation support the body's natural defense mechanisms, helping to strengthen the immune response and promote overall health.

5.1.4 Regulated Body Temperature: Regular practice of Tummo techniques can have an impact on the body's ability to regulate temperature. Practitioners may develop a greater capacity to withstand cold temperatures, as the inner heat generated provides a natural source of warmth and insulation.

5.2 Mental and Emotional Transformation

Working with the inner fire in Tummo practice also leads to profound shifts in the practitioner's mental and emotional states. Here are some aspects of mental and emotional transformation that can arise:

5.2.1 Heightened Mental Clarity: The cultivation of the inner fire supports mental clarity and focus. As the mind becomes more concentrated and centered, practitioners experience enhanced cognitive function, improved memory, and increased mental acuity.

5.2.2 Emotional Balance: The inner fire generated in Tummo practice has a balancing effect on the emotions. Practitioners may experience a greater sense of emotional stability, reduced reactivity, and an increased ability to observe and understand their emotional states without being overwhelmed by them.

5.2.3 Increased Mindfulness and Presence: Tummo practice cultivates mindfulness and present-moment awareness. As practitioners deepen their connection with the inner fire, they develop an enhanced capacity to stay fully present in the moment, experiencing a profound sense of aliveness and connection with the present reality.

5.2.4 Transformation of Negative Patterns: Working with the inner fire can facilitate the transformation of negative mental and emotional patterns. As practitioners develop a heightened awareness of their thoughts and emotions, they can more effectively recognize and release patterns that no longer serve them, fostering personal growth and positive change.

5.2.5 Spiritual Awakening: The practice of Tummo and the transformation that arises from working with the inner fire can lead to profound spiritual awakening. As practitioners connect with the inner fire and experience the interplay between body, mind, and spirit, they may gain deeper insights into the nature of reality, experience expanded states of consciousness, and foster a sense of interconnectedness with all beings.

Through the physical and mental transformation that occurs in Tummo practice, practitioners can experience increased vitality, improved well-being, heightened mental clarity, emotional balance, and spiritual awakening. It is important to approach these transformative processes with patience, perseverance, and the guidance of qualified teachers to ensure a safe and effective practice.

Chapter 6: Tummo and Spiritual Practices

Tummo, with its focus on the cultivation of the inner fire, holds deep connections to spiritual practices and traditions. This chapter explores the relationship between Tummo and various spiritual paths, highlighting the ways in which Tummo can complement and enhance spiritual development.

6.1 Tummo in Tibetan Buddhism

Tummo has a profound significance within Tibetan Buddhist practices. It is considered a form of inner tantra, a practice that combines physical and energetic techniques with meditation and visualization to facilitate spiritual awakening.

Tummo is often associated with the completion

stage practices of Vajrayana and Mahamudra, where the inner fire is utilized as a transformative force to realize the nature of mind and achieve enlightenment.

Within Tibetan Buddhism, Tummo practice is often integrated into the broader path of meditation, ethics, and wisdom teachings. It serves as a powerful method to purify negative mental and emotional patterns, balance the subtle energy system, and awaken the innate wisdom and compassion within practitioners.

6.2 Tummo in Yogic Traditions

Tummo practice also shares similarities with certain yogic traditions, particularly those that focus on the awakening of Kundalini energy. Kundalini, often depicted as a dormant serpent coiled at the base of the spine, represents the latent spiritual energy within an individual. Through specific practices, including breath control, visualization, and meditation, Kundalini is awakened and ascends through the central energy channel, leading to spiritual awakening and union with the divine.

In yogic traditions, Tummo practices align with the awakening and ascent of Kundalini energy, as the inner fire generated in Tummo practice is believed to activate and guide the movement of Kundalini. This alignment can facilitate spiritual transformation, expansion of consciousness, and the realization of higher states of being.

6.3 Tummo and Energy Healing Modalities

The cultivation of the inner fire in Tummo practice resonates with various energy healing modalities found across different spiritual and cultural traditions. These modalities recognize the vital role of energy flow in maintaining physical, emotional, and spiritual well-being.

By working with the inner fire, Tummo practitioners develop a heightened awareness of subtle energy and the ability to manipulate its flow. This understanding aligns with practices such as Reiki, Qi Gong, and Pranic Healing, where the manipulation of energy is used to restore balance, remove blockages, and support healing on all levels.

6.4 Tummo and Mind-Body Connection

Tummo practice emphasizes the profound connection between the mind and the body. The cultivation of the inner fire involves the integration of breath, visualization, and meditation, which harness the power of the mind to influence and transform the body's energy system.

This mind-body connection is a central principle in various spiritual practices, including mindfulness, meditation, and somatic practices. Tummo enhances this connection, allowing practitioners to experience a deep integration of body and mind,

fostering a holistic approach to spiritual

development.

6.5 Tummo as a Path of Self-Realization

Ultimately, Tummo can be seen as a path of self-

realization, encompassing physical, mental, and

spiritual dimensions. By harnessing the inner fire

and engaging in Tummo practices, individuals

embark on a transformative journey of self-discovery and self-mastery.

Tummo facilitates the exploration of one's inner landscape, awakening dormant potentials, and unveiling the inherent wisdom and luminosity of the true self. It serves as a vehicle for personal and spiritual growth, leading to a deeper understanding of one's purpose, interconnectedness with all beings, and the realization of ultimate truth.

Incorporating Tummo into spiritual practices provides a powerful framework for self-transformation, spiritual evolution, and the attainment of profound states of consciousness. It is essential to approach these practices with reverence, proper guidance, and respect for one's individual capacities and limitations.

Chapter 7: Preparing for Tummo Practice

Before embarking on the practice of Tummo, it is important to make adequate preparations to ensure a safe and effective experience. This chapter explores the essential steps and considerations for preparing oneself for Tummo practice.

7.1 Physical Preparedness

Preparing the physical body is crucial for engaging in Tummo practice. Here are some key aspects of physical preparedness:

7.1.1 Physical Fitness: Engaging in regular physical exercise and maintaining overall physical fitness is beneficial for Tummo practice. Strengthening the body, improving flexibility, and enhancing cardiovascular health can support the practice and help to withstand the demands of intense energy work.

7.1.2 Breath Awareness: Developing an awareness of the breath is important as breath control plays a significant role in Tummo practice. Prioritize learning and practicing deep, diaphragmatic breathing techniques to cultivate breath awareness and enhance the ability to manipulate and direct the breath.

7.1.3 Posture and Alignment: Cultivate a stable and comfortable posture for meditation and energy work. Whether sitting cross-legged on the floor or using a chair, ensure proper spinal alignment and relaxed yet alert body posture to support the flow of energy during Tummo practice.

7.2 Mental and Emotional Readiness

Preparing the mind and emotions is equally important for engaging in Tummo practice. Here are some considerations for mental and emotional readiness:

7.2.1 Clear Intentions: Clarify your intentions for engaging in Tummo practice. Reflect on why you are drawn to this practice and what you hope to achieve. Establishing clear intentions can provide focus, motivation, and a sense of purpose throughout the journey.

7.2.2 Emotional Stability: Cultivate emotional stability and resilience to navigate the various experiences that may arise during Tummo practice. Develop mindfulness and emotional awareness, allowing for the recognition and acceptance of emotions without being overwhelmed by them.

7.2.3 Patience and Persistence: Tummo practice requires patience and persistence. Understand that progress may be gradual, and experiences can vary from person to person. Cultivate a mindset of perseverance, trust in the process, and a willingness to commit to regular practice.

7.3 Environmental Considerations

Creating a conducive environment for Tummo practice enhances the overall experience. Consider the following environmental factors:

7.3.1 Quiet Space: Find a quiet and peaceful space for practice where you can minimize external distractions. This can support deep concentration, inner exploration, and the cultivation of stillness within.

7.3.2 Proper Ventilation: Ensure the practice space is well-ventilated to allow for fresh air circulation. This helps maintain a comfortable body temperature during intense energy work and prevents feelings of suffocation or discomfort.

7.3.3 Temperature Regulation: Adjust the room temperature to a comfortable level that allows for optimal practice. As Tummo practice involves generating inner heat, it is important to strike a balance between a warm enough environment to support the practice and avoiding excessive heat that may lead to discomfort or dehydration.

7.4 Teacher and Guidance

Seeking guidance from an experienced teacher or mentor is highly recommended when undertaking Tummo practice. A qualified teacher can provide proper instruction, guidance, and support throughout the journey, ensuring that the practice is approached in a safe and effective manner.

7.4.1 Finding a Teacher: Research and seek out reputable teachers or schools that specialize in Tummo practice or related disciplines such as Tibetan Buddhism or Kundalini Yoga. Look for teachers who have a solid background, experience, and a genuine lineage in the practice.

7.4.2 Learning in a Traditional Setting: Consider the possibility of learning Tummo in a traditional setting, such as a retreat or a monastery. Immersing oneself in a dedicated practice environment can provide a deeper understanding of the practice and foster a stronger connection with its lineage and cultural context.

7.4.3 Regular Check-ins and Support: Establish a regular communication channel with your teacher or mentor. Regular check-ins can help address questions, clarify doubts, and receive guidance on refining your practice. This ongoing support ensures that you progress safely and effectively on your Tummo journey.

By adequately preparing oneself physically, mentally, emotionally, and environmentally, and seeking guidance from a qualified teacher, individuals can create a solid foundation for engaging in Tummo practice. These preparations lay the groundwork for a transformative and enriching experience.

Chapter 8: Conclusion

The practice of Tummo, with its focus on cultivating the inner fire, offers a transformative journey of self-discovery, spiritual awakening, and physical and mental evolution. Throughout this guide, we have explored the origins, significance, techniques, benefits, and spiritual aspects of

Tummo practice. As we conclude, let us recap the key points and reflect on the essence of Tummo.

Tummo, also known as "inner fire" or "fierce breath," is deeply rooted in Tibetan Buddhist practices, where it is regarded as a potent method for physical, mental, and spiritual transformation. The concept of inner fire represents the innate energy within us, and Tummo practice harnesses this energy through specific breath control methods, visualization, and meditation.

By engaging in Tummo practice, practitioners can experience profound benefits. Physically, Tummo practice increases body heat, improves energy circulation, enhances the immune system, and regulates body temperature. Mentally and emotionally, it promotes mental clarity, emotional balance, mindfulness, and transformation of negative patterns. Moreover, Tummo practice holds spiritual significance, aligning with Tibetan Buddhist practices, yogic traditions, energy healing modalities, and the exploration of the mind-body connection.

To embark on the Tummo journey, adequate preparations are necessary. Physical preparedness through fitness, breath awareness, and posture; mental and emotional readiness with clear intentions, emotional stability, patience, and persistence; and creating a conducive practice environment are essential considerations. Seeking guidance from a qualified teacher or mentor ensures a safe and effective practice, providing instruction, support, and the opportunity to learn in a traditional setting.

As you embark on your Tummo practice, remember that it is a personal journey of self-realization and transformation. Embrace the process with dedication, patience, and openness, allowing the inner fire to guide you towards deeper levels of understanding, connection, and spiritual awakening.

May your Tummo practice illuminate the path ahead, igniting the inner fire within and unveiling the vast potential that resides within your being.

May you find joy, clarity, and profound transformation along this sacred journey of Tummo practice.

Om Tare Tuttare Ture Soha.

Printed in Great Britain
by Amazon